Genie in my Drink Bottle

and Other Fun Writing Prompts

Written by Melissa Gijsbers

i

Dedication

To all the young writers that attend writers' group and encourage me to keep coming up with fun writing prompts.

Table of Contents

Introduction

Welcome writers,

Creative writing is a lot of fun, and to get started is through writing prompts. Writing prompts are designed to be a starting point for your imagination. Once you've started, you're free to let your writing take you anywhere you like!

Have fun with the prompts in this book, and try out different styles of writing—fiction, non-fiction, poetry, play, blog post, or something completely different.

You might like to mix things up by writing some stories in first person and others in third person. You may even want to try some poetry or a genre you haven't written before. Remember, writing prompts don't have to be taken literally. You may find that these prompts inspire stories that head in completely unexpected directions.

When you are writing, don't worry too much about your first draft not being perfect. You can fix up any spelling or grammatical mistakes in your next draft. That is what editing is for.

I hope you enjoy these writing prompts.

Happy Writing!

Melissa Gijsbers

Melissa's Golden Rules of Writing

1. **Have FUN!** - creative writing is all about the process. After all, if you're not having fun, what's the point?

2. **It's YOUR Story**—write your story your way. There is no single way to write a story, so experiment, play, and write whatever comes to mind.

3. **Experiment**—play with different styles and genre. You never know what you'll enjoy writing until you try. Plus, you don't have to limit yourself to just one type of writing.

4. **Try something new**—if your story isn't working, try something new. A different point of view, style, genre, or even a new prompt if the one you're working on isn't working!

5. **Have FUN!** - Did I mention have fun? Whether you

are writing something silly or serious, creating a story is fun, so enjoy it.

6. **Write as long or as short as you like**—If you only have a few minutes, then you can write something short. It doesn't matter if you don't finish a story or piece of writing in a sitting, or at all.

7. **First drafts are meant to be crappy***—this is something many people don't realise, it's no issue if your first draft is not perfect. Everything can be fixed up in the editing process.

8. **You don't have to finish**—if you're writing for fun, and you don't finish your story, that's okay. You can always come back and finish it another time.

9. **Have FUN!** - I may have mentioned this before… have fun writing your story, poem, or whatever else you're writing.

* Crappy = flawed, imperfect, incomplete, not up to scratch, unsatisfactory

Tips on how to use Writing Prompts

1. **Read the prompt carefully**— What is it asking you to do?

2. **Think outside the box**— Is there a way you can use the prompt in a fun or unusual way?

3. **Use the prompt more than once**— If you have more than one idea, then write them down. You can use a prompt in many different ways

4. **Just write**— Don't worry about titles, spelling, grammar, or anything else, just write. This is a first draft. Underline any words you're not sure about spelling and you can come back to them later. Everything can be fixed up in the editing process

5. **Read over what you've written**— When you've done, read over what you've written and fix up any obvious errors. Then you can have fun editing your story to share (if you want to).

Writing Prompts

1

Write a story about the day your

parents go on strike!

2

You find yourself on a brand-new reality TV show, write a story about your time on the show.

3

Write a story about a technology disaster that turns out to be the best thing that could have happened.

4

You are bored, so you make a box car out of an old cardboard box. When you get in, you are transported on a magical adventure. Write a story about your trip.

5

Write a story about unconventional pirates

6

Write a story about unusual
animals on a train.

7

Write a story about a disaster in the

kitchen.

8

It's the year 3535. You discover a jar of Vegemite. Write a story about your discovery.

9

Write a story about a mysterious leak/leek.

10

Write a story about the day you wake
up on the wrong side of the bed.

11

You are a matchmaker. Write a story about finding the perfect match

12

You carry around a water bottle with you everywhere. One day, you discover a genie in your water bottle! Write a story about the genie in your water bottle.

13

Write a story about an afternoon tea
where nothing goes quite to plan.

14

Write the back story of a fictional villain.

15

A letter arrives address to you, dated 100 years ago. Who is the letter from and what does it say?

16

Choose a random object
You are an alien who must describe
this item and what it does to your
superiors. Write a copy of your
report.

17

Write a story featuring Teddy Bear shaped Biscuits.

18

You start playing a game, and next thing you know you're inside the game! Write a story about your experience and how you get back home again.

19

Your family has a secret—you go on holiday through a secret portal! Write a story about what REALLY happened during the school holidays.

20

For your birthday, you are given a gift card to a strange shop you've never heard of before: *The Dancing Robot Market*. Write a story about spending your gift card.

21

You are out walking and pick up
what you think is an ordinary stick.
Imagine your surprise when you
discover the stick is actually a magic
wand! Write a story about what
happens next.

22

Write a story about digging a hole.

23

Write a story about what happens to
our thoughts when they're forgotten.

24

Pick a random object
You are now a burglar and that
random object is the only thing you
steal. Write a story about your
exploits.

25

Write a fairy tale from the point of
view of one of the minor characters.

26

Write a story using these random words: Balloon, Unicorn, Coffee table, Mountain, Orange.

27

Write a story about how musical instruments feel when they are being played.

28

Pick a random object.
This is now the key to a murder
mystery.

29

Write a story where unicorns are the
main form of transport

30

Write a story featuring a donut.

31

You are practicing your musical instrument. You look up to find that you are now in a stadium playing for a sold out show as either a solo act, or as part of your favourite band. Write a story about your performance.

32

Invent a new gameshow and use this for a setting for a story, or a news article announcing this amazing new TV show.

33

It's Book Week and you dress up as your favourite book character ready for the parade at school. Instead of walking in the parade, you end up inside the book! Write a story about your adventure and how you get home again.

34

You invent a robot to help you clean your room… but things don't go to plan. Write a story about your invention and what happens when your robot starts cleaning your room.

35

Write a story about building a
sandcastle.

36

Write a story about a backwards day
– a day that starts with dinner and
ends with breakfast. What happens
during this backwards day?

37

Choose a random object.
Use this object to write a story about
the superhero's assistant or sidekick.
The object could be the sidekick, or
inspire your character.

38

You are playing your favourite
sport, and the coach brings in a
substitute player – a dragon!
Write a story about what
happens next.

39

Write a story about a magical pair of

shoes.

40

You open a door and, instead of finding yourself in the next room, you find yourself in a magical land. Write a story about your adventure, and how you get home again.

41

Write a story about what your teddy
bear and other toys get up to when
you're not around.

42

You are running late for something important. Write a story about why you are running late!

43

Write a story about an unusual
birthday party.

44

You see a t-shirt with an interesting pattern. On closer inspection, the pattern on the top comes to life! Write a story about what happens.

45

Write a story about who would win an epic battle between two dinosaurs.

46

Write a story about the creature who lives inside the fridge that decides what food should go off!

47

One day, a dragon decides to follow you home. Write a story about convincing your family to keep your new pet.

48

Write a story about the real reason
the tooth fairy is late to leave money
for a tooth.

49

You are moving house and when you start unpacking, you find something unexpected in one of the boxes. What have you found and how does it change your life?

50

A mysterious note is pushed under your door. The only problem is, this is a cupboard door and not a door to the outside! What does the note say, and what happens next?

51

Write a non-romantic love story.

52

Write a story about the monster
under your bed.

Conclusion

I hope you've had fun with these writing prompts and enjoyed crafting stories with them.

One fantastic thing about writing prompts is that, you can use them more than once and come out with an entirely different story.

If you do want to use the prompt again and aren't quite sure what to do, try writing from a different point of view, or a different style or genre than you did last time.

Try it and see what happens.

You can use these prompts over and over to have fun with your imagination.

Happy Writing,

Melissa Gijsbers.

Author Bio

Melissa Gijsbers is an author and booklover. She started working with young writers in 2013 at the Monash Public Library and has been inspiring them to write by providing them with crazy writing prompts ever since! In 2020, the writers' groups went online and inspired young writers around Australia to have fun with their imaginations.

She currently lives in the Latrobe Valley in Victoria, Australia and spends quite a bit of time coming up with fun writing ideas for stories, as well as writing more books herself.

You can find out more about Melissa on her website— www.melissagijsbers.com

Acknowledgements

First, I'd like to acknowledge all the young writers from around Australia who attended Virtual Writers' Groups during lockdowns in 2020 and 2021. We were able to find moments of joy through creative writing and sharing stories with each other.

Second, to Eileen Louden, Peter McGarry, and all the librarians at the Monash Public Library Service for starting me working with young writers in 2013. Look what you started!

Third, to my kids, Nat and Zac, for endless hours putting up with me trying out writing prompts on them before presenting them writers' groups and doing their best to hide their eye rolls (yes, I did see them).